E S T A T E   P U B L I C A T I O N S

NEWQUAY · PERRANPORTH
ST COLUMB MAJOR · ST MAWGAN · TRENA

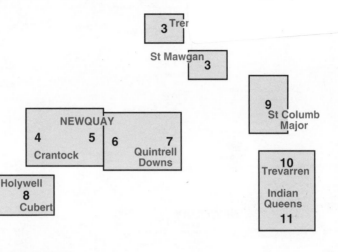

3 Tren

St Mawgan **3**

9 St Columb Major

NEWQUAY
4 **5** **6** **7**
Crantock Quintrell Downs

Holywell
8
Cubert

10
Trevarren

Indian
Queens
11

PERRANPORTH **12** **12** Goonhavern

ROAD MAP	**Page 2**
INDEX TO STREETS	**Page 13**

Scale of street plans: 4 Inches to 1 Mile (unless otherwise stated)

▬▬▬ Motorway	Every effort has been made to verify the accuracy of information in this book but the publishers cannot accept responsibility for expense or loss caused by an error or omission. Information that will be of assistance to the user of the maps will be welcomed.	〜 Stream / River
▬ 'A' Road / Dual		Canal
▬ 'B' Road / Dual		→ One-way Street
▬ Minor Road / Dual		🄿 Car Park
▬ Track		🄲 Public Convenience
▨ Pedestrianized	The representation on these maps of a road, track or path is no evidence of the existence of a right of way.	🄸 Tourist Information
▬■▬ Railway / Station		✚ Place of Worship
- - - Footpath		● Post Office

Street plans prepared and published by ESTATE PUBLICATIONS, Bridewell House, TENTERDEN, KENT.
The Publishers acknowledge the co-operation of the local authorities
of towns represented in this atlas.

OS Ordnance Survey® This product includes mapping data licensed from Ordnance Survey®
with the permission of the Controller of Her Majesty's Stationery Office.

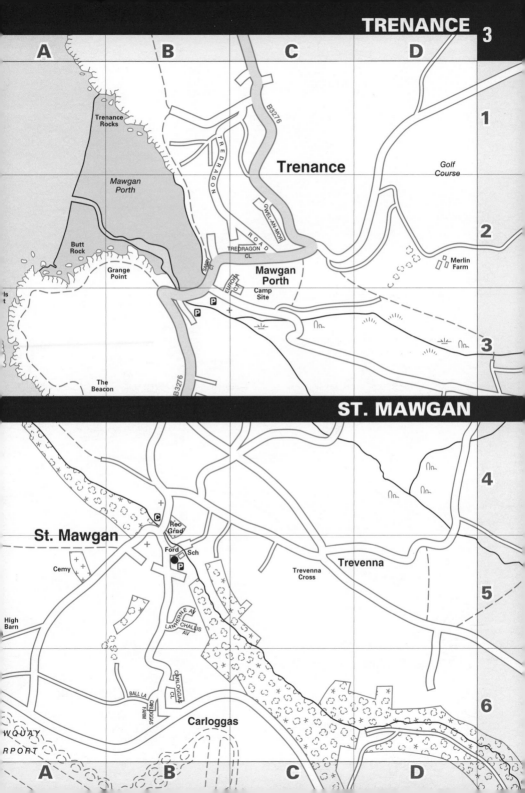

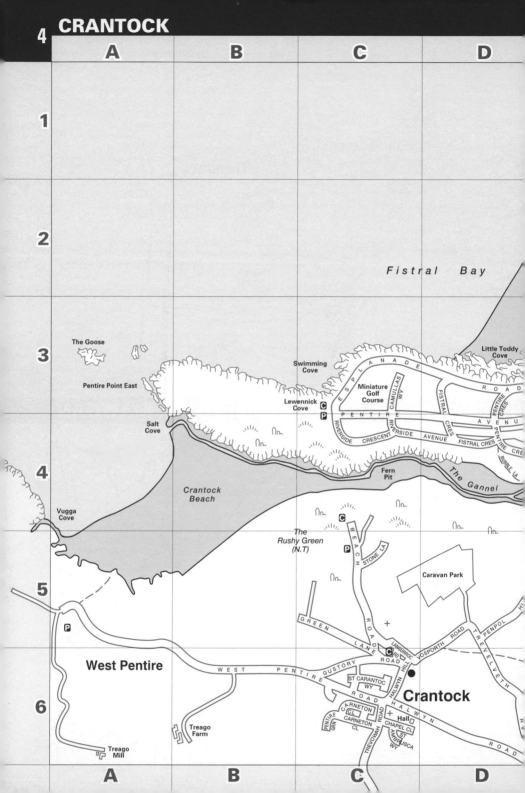

E   F   G   H

Towan Head

Spy Cove

Hedge Cove

Seal Hole

Old Dane

Newquay Bay

Hotel

Fistral
Beach

The
Beacon

KING EDWARD CRES

DANE RD

HEADLAND ROAD

Pigeon
Cove

NEWQUAY

Fly Cove

North Pier

Tolcarne
Beach

Tolcarne
Point

Golf Links

BELMONT
PL
ACLANDO

SYDNEY RD

NTH QUAY HILL

FERNHILL

South
Pier

Towan
Beach

The
Island

Great Western
Beach

NEWQUAY

HILL

NARROWCLIFF

CLIFF RD

COLVREATH RD

ULALIA ROAD

EDGCUMBE GDS

ELIOZ GARDENS

HOLYWELL
RD

QUARRY PK RD

EDGCUMBE AV

Trethellan

Super-
store

FISTRAL TER

GOLF
TER
TREFOSE
AV

HOPE
TER

JUBILEE ST

ST PIRANS
ST

MANOR RD

WESLEY RD

Trevena   Alma

BEACH RD

BANK ST

CRESCENT

TOWN PROM

Sea
Life
Centre

ISLAND CRES

TREBARWITH CRES

EAST   STREET

STA PAR

TOLCARNE RD

OAKLEIGH TER

SPRING FIELD RD

BERRY RD

EDGCUMBE AV

PENTIRE   ROAD

CRANTOCK ST

Cerny

HIGHER TOWER RD

ST CUTH
-BERTS
RD

ST MARYS
RD

TREFFRY

MANOR

ST MICHAELS

WISE

ST GEORGES RD

JENNORS RD

ROAD

MARCUS HILL

SEYMOUR AV

GROSVENOR AV

ST THOMAS

ROBARTES
RD

TOR

CARCLEW

PARGOLLA ROAD

TRENANCE

TRETHELLAN HILL

ATLANTIC RD

MOUNT

PENTIRE
CRES

BEZANT
CL

POLVELLA
CL

CURLEW CL

PARC
GODREVY

TREVEAN

PENMERE
DRIVE

PENMERE DR

GANNEL ROAD

WINDSOR
CT

REEDS

TREGUNNEL HILL

Football
Ground

Fire
Sta

CLEVEDON

BRACKEN
TERRACE

Sch

MAYFIELD RD

VIVIAN RD

TRENARTH

PENMERIN RD

LANHENVOR AV

BAY VW TER

HEADLEIGH RD

TRENANCE AV

HOSP

Gdns

Mus

Trenance Leisure
Lido & Water

Trenance Chalet
& Caravan Park

CHYNANCE   DRIVE

LISTRY
RD

LISTRY RD

TREMBATH
CRES

CHIVERTON

TRETHEWEY WAY

TREGUNNEL HILL

ESTUARY
VW

MORRIS
GDNS

OLD BARN
CT

PENGANNEL
CL

AGAR RD

CHEVIOT RD

HAWKINS ROAD

RAWLEY LANE

LINDEN AV

CLIFDEN AV

ANTHONY
CL

TREDOUR ROAD

TRENANCE   LANE

LINDEN CRES

TREVEMPER RD

EDGCUMBE AV

TRENINNIC CL

GOON VREA RD

TREFORDA RD

TREWERTH RD

HILL

Sch

River Gannel

WAY

GANNEL

ROAD

Trenance

TREVEMPER   ROAD

MELLANVRANE LANE

CHICHESTER CRES

TREVEMPER
RD

GRESHAM CL

MIDDLETON
RD

GOON
PENNA

PENNA

WYCH HAZEL
WAY

ELM CLOSE

DALE

KEV

TR

MEA
SITE

Little Trevithick

Treringey
Round

Trevemper

Treringey

A392

A39

E   F   G   H

E F G H

A3059

1

Tregenna

Treloy

2

St. Columb
Minor

PRIORY ROAD

TON HEIGHTS

PEMBROKE RD

CALSHOT CLOSE

Cemy

ALTON ROAD

Rialton
Barton

QUINTRELL ROAD

3

HOOL

Trewollack
Farm

4

Bejowan

Chapel

5

QUINTRELL
DOWNS

Quintrell
Downs

NORTH WY

ROAD

WEST ROAD EAST

QUINTRELL GDNS

A392

ROAD

6

WILLOW CL

VYVYAN DRIVE

TRETHIGGEY CRES

SOUTH WAY

A3058

GARDEN WY

LITTLE TRETHIGGEY

Reservoir

E F G H

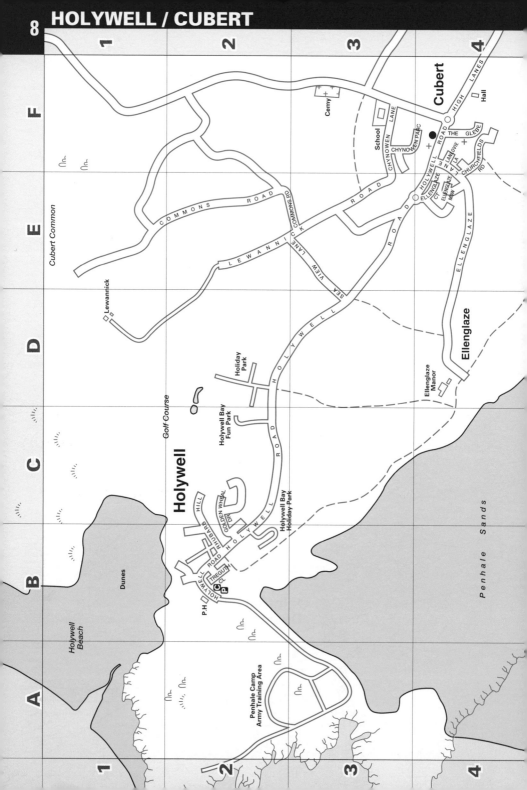

Cubert

Hall

Cemy

School

CHYNOWEN LANE

CHYNOWEN PARC

CHYNOWEN LANE

THE GLEBE

HIGH LANES

HOLYWELL ROAD

ELLENGLAZE

ELLENGLAZE CT

ELLENGLAZE LA

MRW

LANOWE

CHURCHFIELDS RD

COMMONS ROAD

CUBECK COMMONS RD

LEWANNICK LANE

SEA VIEW LANE

ROAD

ROAD

Cubert Common

Lewannick

Ellenglaze

Ellenglaze Manor

HOLYWELL ROAD

Golf Course

Holiday Park

Holywell Bay Fun Park

Holywell

HILL

GOLDEN WHEAL

RIBBA DR

HOLYWELL ROAD

Holywell Bay Holiday Park

TREGUTH CL

HOLYWELL ROAD

P.H

Dunes

Holywell Beach

Penhale Camp Army Training Area

Penhale Sands

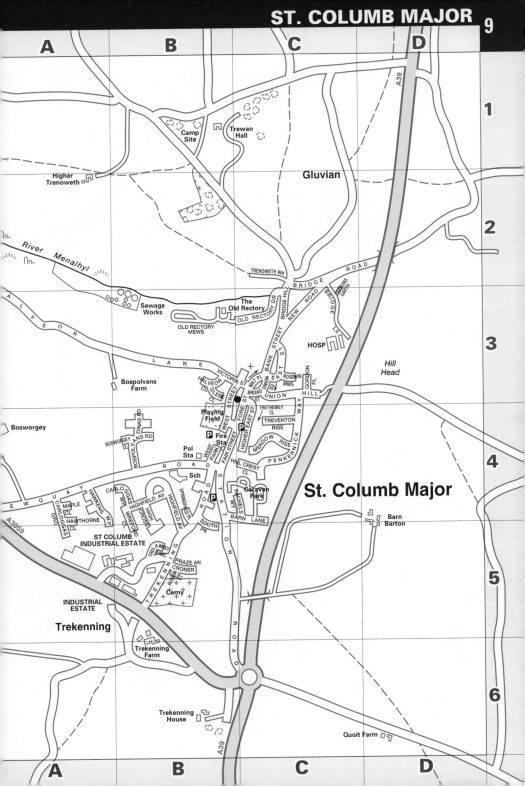

Ruthvoes

Penrose Farm

LODGE WY

HANOVER PARC

WARREN RD

Indian Queens Workshops

Pony Centre

Treliver

Blackcross

Trevarren

St. Columb Road

FRANCIS

CARWOL

PEAR GRN

TREMEAR GRN

PARKA

PARKA

ST. COLUMB ROAD

NEWQUAY

A39

A39

A392

A30

A30

ROAD

PORTLAND

SAINT FRANCIS

Indian Queens
Fraddon
Higher Fraddon

Fraddon Down

STAMPS HILL

River Fal

Trerice Farm

Wheal Remfry China Clay Works
Clay Pit

B3279

Carvengan Manor

KEAST GATE HILL

POCOHONTAS CRES
BARNFIELD TER

Sch
OCEAN VIEW (SMALL FOREST ESTATE)
CHAPEL CT
PRINCESS X
QUEENS TER

HEATHER MEADOW

CHAPEL LANE

ROAD
ARKA

HARVENNA CL

BARTON LANE

Harvenna Farm

Polmenna Farm

Village Hall

MY LORDS RD
KING
WESTBOURNE TER
PENHALE GDNS

Travel Inn

Trewheela Farm

NEW ROAD
A30
B3275

PERRANPORTH

A   B   C   D

Reen Sands

Golf Course

Droskyn
Point

1

Droskyn
Point

Cliff Road

Tregundy
CT

P

C

THE PROMENADE

BEACH

PONSMERE

SANDY BAY
HOLIDAY FLATS

Liby

EUREKA

JERRY
DAVEY
CL

JOSEPHS

HANOVER

St PIRIANS RD

STATION

i

ST PIRIANS ROAD

RAMOTH WAY

B3285

BUDNIC HILL

REEN MANOR LANE

WHEAL CATHERINE CL

P C

Rec Grnd

BUDNICK

Droskyn Way

CT

Tregundy Road

ROAD

Fuller Rd

TYWARNHAYLE

LWR TYWARNHAYLE

HANOVER CT

GOWER

ST GEORGES HILL

BEACH RD

BOSCAWEN ROAD

WHEAL

LEISURE

Fire
Sta

LEISURE

WHEAL

ROAD

Nature
Reserve

PERRANPORTH

2

WY

TREBISKIN

TRENINNICK

HILL CT

ST GEORGES VW

HIGHER BOLENNA

COOMBE

TYWARNHAYLE

TRELAWNEY RD

MINERS CT

SEINERS

+

Playing
Field

LISKEY HILL CRES

WHEAL

LA

SUNNYSIDE

TREVAN

GRANNYS St MICHAELS ROAD

ENSILVA

LAMORE

LISKEY HILL

RIDGEWAY

STATION RD
INDUSTRIAL
ESTATE

Police
Sta

ROAD NEW

B3285

ST COOMBE VW

BOLENNA LA

NAMPARA
CT

GRANNYS
LANE

SOMERVILLE
RD

Sch

Nansmellyn
Farm

PERRAN LA

Nampara

WELWAY

BOLINGEY ROAD

CHAPEL HILL

ROAD

REEN HILL

3

B3284

LISKEY HILL

MILL ROAD

Bolingey

GOONHAVERN

A   B   C   D

B3285

Rose

St Pirans
Round

A3075

4

JUBILEE TER

Newperran
Tourist
Park

ROAD

A3075

5

Reen
Cross

Rosehill

TREBARTHEN TER

Rec
Grnd

Roseville
Holiday
Park

ROSE MEADOW$

MARTYNS CL

NEWQUAY ROAD

School

NEWQUAY

HALT

Garden
Centre

Carn Moor

Nature
Reserve

Goonhavern

ROAD

CARRIAGE
PARC

BRIDGE

C

POLLARDS ROAD

FIR CL

**GOONHAVERN
IND EST**

6

A3075

NEWQUAY

FIR CL

Caravan
Site

ROAD

B3285

World in
Miniature

A   B   C   D

A - Z INDEX TO STREETS
with Postcodes

Newquay Rd,	
St Columb Rd TR9	10 A3
Newquay Rd,	
St Columb TR9	9 A4
Newquay Rd, Truro TR4	12 B6
North Quay Hill TR7	5 F2
North Way TR8	7 F5
Oakleigh Ter TR7	5 H3
Ocean Vw TR9	11 B5
Old Barn Ct TR7	5 F5
Old Rectory Dr TR9	9 C3
Parc Godrevy TR7	5 E4
Pargolla Rd TR7	5 H3
Parka Rd TR9	10 B4
Parkenbutts TR7	6 D1
Parkland Cl TR7	6 D2
Parsons Garth TR9	9 C3
Pear Gn TR9	10 B4
Pembroke Rd TR7	7 E2
Pendragon Cres TR7	6 A5
Pengannel Cl TR7	5 G5
Penhale Gdns TR9	11 A7
Penhallow Rd TR7	6 C1
Penina Av TR7	5 H5
Penkernick Way TR9	9 C4
Penmere Dr TR7	5 E4
Penmerrin Cres TR7	5 H4
Penpol Hill TR8	4 D5
Pensilva TR6	12 B2
Pentire Av TR7	4 C4
Pentire Cres TR7	4 D4
Pentire Grn TR8	4 C6
Pentire Rd TR7	5 E3
Penwartha Cl TR7	6 D2
Percy Davey Cl TR6	12 B1
Perran Coombe TR6	12 A3
Place Parc TR7	6 D1
Pocohontas Cres TR9	11 C5
Pollards Cl TR4	12 C6
Polvella Cl TR7	5 E4
Polwhele Rd TR7	6 A5
Ponsmere Rd TR6	12 B1
Porth Bean Rd TR7	6 C1
Porth Par TR7	6 C1
Porth Way TR7	6 C2
Praze An Croner TR9	9 B5
Praze Rd TR7	6 B1
Princess Parc TR9	11 C5
Priory Rd TR7	7 E2
Pydar Cl TR7	6 B3
Quarry Park Rd TR7	5 H3
Queens Cl TR9	11 C5
Quintrell Gdns TR8	7 G6
Quintrell Rd TR7	7 E3
Rachels Way TR9	9 B4
Ramoth Way TR6	12 C1
Rawley La TR7	5 H4
Reeds Way TR7	5 F4
Reen Hill TR6	12 D3
Reen Manor La TR6	12 D1
Rhubarb Hill TR8	8 B2
Rialton Heights TR7	7 E2
Rialton Rd TR7	7 E3
Ridgeway TR6	12 B2
Riverside Av TR7	4 C4
Riverside Cres TR7	4 C4

Robartes Rd TR7	5 H4
Roma Ct TR7	6 C2
Rose Mdws TR4	12 C5
Rosewin Mews TR9	9 C3
Rubble La TR7	4 D4
Ruskin Ct TR9	9 B5
St Ambrusca Way TR8	4 C6
St Annes Rd TR7	6 A2
St Aubyn Cres TR7	6 A3
St Carantoc Way TR8	4 C6
St Cuthberts Rd TR7	5 F3
St Francis Rd TR9	10 B4
St Georges Hill TR6	12 A3
St Georges Hill Cl TR6	12 A2
St Georges Rd TR7	5 F3
St Johns Rd TR7	5 F4
St Marys Rd TR7	5 F3
St Michaels Rd,	
Perranporth TR6	12 B2
St Michaels Rd,	
Newquay TR7	5 F4
St Pirans Rd TR7	5 F3
St Pirians Rd TR6	12 B1
St Thomas Rd TR7	5 H3
Sandy Bay Holiday Flats	
TR6	12 B1
Sandy Ct TR8	3 B2
School Cl TR7	7 E3
Sea View La TR8	8 D3
Seiners Cl TR6	12 B2
Seymour Av TR7	5 G3
Shackleton Dr TR7	6 B3
Somerville Rd TR6	12 B3
South Pk TR9	9 B4
South Quay Hill TR7	5 F2
South Way TR8	7 F6
Springfield Pl TR9	9 B4
Springfield Rd TR7	5 H3
Stafford Cl TR7	6 D2
Stamps Hill TR9	11 D5
Stanharver Cl TR7	7 E2
Stanways Rd TR7	6 D2
Station Par TR7	5 H3
Station Rd,	
Perranporth TR6	12 B1
Station Rd,	
St Columb TR9	9 B4
Stone La TR8	4 C5
Suncrest Est TR9	11 B5
Sunnyside TR6	12 B2
Sweet Briar Cres TR7	6 A5
Sydney Rd TR7	5 F3
Tamarisk La TR7	6 A5
The Crescent TR7	5 G3
The Drang TR9	10 C4
The Glebe TR8	8 F4
The Gounce TR6	12 B1
The Promenade TR6	12 B1
The Rectory Mews TR9	9 B3
Toby Way TR7	5 F2
Tolcarne Mews TR7	5 H3
Tolcarne Rd TR7	5 H3
Tor Rd TR7	5 H3
Towan Blystra Rd TR7	6 A3
Tower Rd TR7	5 F3
Town Prom TR7	5 G3
Trebarthen Ter TR4	12 B5
Trebarwith Cres TR7	5 G3

Tredinnick Way TR6	12 A2
Tredour Rd TR7	5 G5
Tredragon Cl TR8	3 B2
Tredragon Rd TR8	3 B1
Treffry Ct TR7	5 F3
Treforda Rd TR7	5 H5
Tregonning Ct*,	
St Pirians Rd TR6	12 B1
Tregoss Rd TR7	5 H3
Tregundy Ct TR6	12 A1
Tregundy Rd TR6	12 A2
Tregunnel Hill TR7	5 F4
Treguth Cl TR8	8 B2
Trekenning Rd TR9	9 B5
Trelawney Parc TR9	9 B5
Treloggan La TR7	6 A5
Treloggan Rd TR7	6 A5
Trembath Cres TR7	5 G4
Tremear Grn TR9	10 B4
Trenance Av TR7	5 H4
Trenance La TR7	5 H5
Trenance Rd TR7	5 H3
Trenarth Rd TR7	5 G4
Trencreek La TR7	6 B4
Trencreek Rd TR7	6 B4
Treninnick Hill TR7	5 H4
Trenoweth Walk TR9	9 C2
Trerice Dr TR7	6 A3
Trethellan Hill TR7	5 E4
Tretherras Cl TR7	6 A3
Tretherras Rd TR7	6 A3
Trethewey Cl TR9	9 C4
Trethewey Way TR7	5 F4
Trethiggey Cres TR8	7 F6
Trevalga Cl*,	
St Michaels Rd TR6	12 B2
Trevean Way TR7	5 E4
Trevelveth Rd TR8	4 D5
Trevemper Rd TR7	5 H5
Trevena Ter TR7	5 F3
Trevenson Rd TR7	6 B3
Treventon Rise TR9	9 C4
Trevian Cl TR6	12 B2
Treviglas Cl TR7	6 D2
Trevithick Cl TR7	5 H5
Trevose Av TR7	5 F3
Trevowah Rd TR8	4 C6
Trewlawney Rd TR7	5 G4
Tuckers Cl TR7	6 B4
Tywarnhayle Rd TR6	12 A2
Ulalia Rd TR7	6 A2
Union Hill TR9	9 C3
Union Sq TR9	9 C3
Upper Hillcrest TR6	12 A2
Veor Rd TR7	6 C2
Victoria St TR9	9 B3
Vivian Cl TR7	5 G4
Vosporth Rd TR8	4 C6
Vyvyan Dr TR8	7 F6
Wainsway TR6	12 B2
Warren Rd TR9	10 D4
Well Way TR7	6 C2
Welway TR6	12 B3
Wesley Yd TR7	5 F3
West Pentire Rd TR8	4 B6
West Pk TR9	9 B4
West Rd TR8	7 E6

West St TR9	9 E
Westbourne Ter TR9	11 A
Wheal Catherine Cl TR6	12 C
Wheal Leisure TR6	12 E
Wheal Leisure Cl*,	
Wheal Leisure TR6	12 B
Wheatfield Cres TR7	6 A
Whitegate Rd TR7	6 A
Wildflower La TR7	6 A
Willow Cl TR8	7 F
Windsor Ct TR7	5 F
Wreford Cl TR9	9 B
Wych Hazel Way TR7	5 H

For an up-to-date publication list and latest prices visit our web site at

www.estate-publications.co.uk

Use the search facility to find the village, town or city you require.

Local Red Books (selection of)

Ashford & Tenterden
Barnstaple & Ilfracombe
Basildon & Billericay
Basingstoke & Andover
Bath & Bradford-upon-Avon
Bedford
Brentwood
Bromley (London Borough)
Burton-upon-Trent & Swadlincote
Cambridge
Chelmsford, Braintree & Maldon
Chester
Chesterfield
Chichester & Bognor Regis
Colchester & Clacton
Crewe
Eastbourne, Bexhill, Seaford & Newhaven
Exeter & Exmouth
Fareham & Gosport
Folkestone, Dover, Deal & Romney Marsh
Gloucester & Cheltenham
Gravesend & Dartford
Great Yarmouth & Lowestoft
Hereford
Ipswich & Felixstowe
Kidderminster

Kingston-upon-Hull
Lancaster & Morecambe
Lincoln
Macclesfield & Wilmslow
Maidstone
Medway & Gillingham
Newport & Chepstow
Northampton
Norwich
Oxford & Abingdon
Peterborough
Plymouth, Saltash & Torpoint
Reading & Henley-on-Thames
Redditch & Bromsgrove
Rugby
Salisbury, Amesbury & Wilton
Sevenoaks
Southend-on-Sea
Stafford
Swindon
Telford
Tunbridge Wells & Tonbridge
Warwick & Royal Leamington Spa
Weston-super-Mare & Clevedon
Winchester
York

Super Red Books

Birmingham (Colour)
Bournemouth
Brighton
Bristol
Cardiff
Coventry
Derby
Edinburgh
Glasgow
Leicester
Nottingham
Portsmouth
Southampton (Colour)
Stoke-on-Trent
Swansea

County Red Books

Bedfordshire
Berkshire
Buckinghamshire
Cambridgeshire
Cheshire
Cornwall
Derbyshire
Devon
Dorset
Essex
Gloucestershire
Hampshire
Herefordshire
Kent
Leicestershire & Rutland

Lincolnshire
Norfolk
Northamptonshire
Nottinghamshire
Oxfordshire
Shropshire
Somerset
Staffordshire
Suffolk
Surrey
Sussex (East)
Sussex (West)
Wiltshire
Worcestershire

Estate Publications, Bridewell House, Tenterden, Kent, TN30 6EP
Tel: 01580 764225 Fax: 01580 763720